Sports Outreach

Leadership Team

Leadership Teams seek to challenge and train Christians to be active and fully committed followers of Christ, able to reproduce reproducers.

Leadership Team is the companion booklet to *Sports Outreach: Principles and Practice of Successful Sports Ministry.*

Christian Focus Publications publishes books for all ages
Our mission statement -

STAYING FAITHFUL
In dependence upon God we seek to help make his infallible word, the Bible, relevant. Our aim is to ensure that the Lord Jesus Christ is presented as the only hope to obtain forgiveness of sin, live a useful life and look forward to heaven with him.

REACHING OUT
Christ's last command requires us to reach out to our world with his gospel. We seek to help fulfill that by publishing books that point people towards Jesus and for them to develop a Christ-like maturity. We aim to equip all levels of readers for life, work ministry and mission.

All rights reserved. No part of this publication may be reproduced, stored in a retrieval system, or transmitted, in any form, by any means, electronic, mechanical, photocopying, recording or otherwise without the prior permission of the publisher or a licence permitting restricted copying. In the U.K. such licences are issued by the Copyright Licensing Agency, 90 Tottenham Court Road, London WIP 9HE.

ISBN 1-85792-872-5

© Copyright Steve Connor 2003

Published in 2003
by
Christian Focus Publications, Ltd.
Geanies House, Fearn, Tain,
Ross-shire, IV20 ITW, Great Britain
www.christianfocus.com

Printed and bound by
J.W. Arrowsmith, Bristol

Cover Design by Alister MacInnes
Illustrations by Graeme Hewitson
Cartoons by Cully
Typeset in BakerSignet and AgencyFB

CONTENTS

Introduction: What's your method? — 4

FOUNDATIONS OF SPORTS MINISTRY
Session 1:
  Why it Works — 6
Session 2:
  Lessons from history — 9
Session 3:
  Biblical Foundations — 11
Session 4:
  Fast Track: Are there any shortcuts? — 14

FIVE PRINCIPLES OF SPORTS MINISTRY
Session 5: Principle 1
  Proclamation: The Verbalisation of Truth — 19
Session 6: Principle 2
  Demonstration: The Visualisation of Truth — 23
Session 7: Principle 3
  Maturation: The Cultivation of Truth — 26
Session 8: Principle 4
  Reproduction: To Reproduce Reproducers — 31
Session 9: Principle 5
  Sportsmanship — 34

STRATEGY FORMATION
Session 10:
  Principles that determine objectives — 37

Conclusion — 41

Memory Verses/Challenge to cut out
and keep with you — 47

Introduction
What's your method?

A man once encountered D L Moody, the famous 19th century evangelist, and said, 'D L Moody, I don't like your method of evangelism.' Moody responded with his characteristic honesty, 'Yes, there are some shortcomings in my method. I'm working to make it better.' Then he asked the man, 'What is your method?'

Taken aback the man replied, 'Why I haven't got one!' Moody responded, 'Well, I still like my method better than yours!'

Every Sunday we see men and women preparing.
Preparing for worship? Preparing to sing praises to the Creator of the universe? Preparing to learn more of His revelation through scripture?
No! They are preparing for athletic competition.
On any given Sunday you will find many of the local churches empty but the sports pitches (fields) packed.

Since we are called to be salt and light, do you have a method of evangelism for those people who love sport but who would never darken the doors of a church?

I hope this booklet will be another step to reach the world of sport – in your sphere of influence – for Christ.

I couldn't think of a better way to start or re-energize your sports ministry than to take a group of potential leaders through the *Sports Outreach Leadership Team*. This is a ten-session companion booklet to *Sports Outreach: Principles and Practice of Successful Sports Ministry*. The *Leadership Team* is designed to train and develop spiritual leadership as well as develop (or re-energise) a sports ministry for your local church. The page numbers referred to in this booklet are in the manual – *Sports Outreach: Principles and Practice*.

Icons for the Bible studies

 **Game Plan:** Aim & desired direction of study.

 **Review**: Reminder of past week's study.

 **Focus**: The current session's particular verses.

 **First Half**: Group/individual questions.

 **Training Tips**: Thought provoking information.

 **Second Half:** Group/individual questions.

 **Instant Replay:** Facts and ideas to consider from the study.

 **SPA:** Spiritual Profile Assessment: A quick way to measure how I am doing and where I am going spiritually. These can be done individually.

 **Action Plan:**
- **A memory verse:** From 'focus verse'.
- **Challenge:** An application for the week.

Session 1: Why it works

Game Plan:
Our aim is to examine the effectiveness of sports ministry.

Focus:
'Therefore, since through God's mercy we have this ministry, we do not lose heart. Rather, we have renounced secret and shameful ways; we do not use deception, nor do we distort the word of God. On the contrary, by setting forth the truth plainly we commend ourselves to every man's conscience in the sight of God' **(2 Cor. 4:1-2).**

First Half:

1. Why is sports ministry so effective?

a.

b.

c.

d.

e.

f.

2. 'A society looking up to athletes as heroes must find heroes looking up to God.' **Wendel Deyo**
In your own words what does that quote mean to you?

3. Why is an athlete less likely to be used effectively in a church than a musician?

4. In your own words, how does sport reach Joe Average?

5. The church is very good at 'playing at home' but sport helps us play 'away'. How does sport help the church play away?

 **Second Half:**

1. Give four examples of how sport shapes our culture.

a.

b.

c.

d.

2. Sport has no generation gaps, this is open to debate, agree or disagree?

3. The number one concern listed under caution of sports ministry (page 23, *Sports Outreach: Principles and Practice*) is no cohesive long term planning. Why is this a danger?

4. Run through the list of 'examining your motives' and give examples of each. Discuss motives for sports ministry.

 **Instant Replay:**
Sports ministry is an effective way to help the church build relationships and share Christ in strategic areas of life. The challenge is not letting sport or sport stars become an idol. In the next session you will learn how the church engaged – disengaged and re-engaged in sports ministry.

Action Plan:

Memory verse:
'Therefore, since through God's mercy we have this ministry, we do not lose heart' **(2 Cor. 4:1-2).**

Challenge:
Consider your community this week and make a list of areas where sports ministry could be effective. Read chapter two of *Sports Outreach: Principles and Practice*.

Session 2: Lessons from history

Game Plan:
Our aim is to examine the development of sport and the effect it has had on the church and society.

Review:
Sports ministry, though it can be very seductive, is one of the best ways the church now has for reaching strategic communities for Christ.

Focus:
'Remember the wonders he has done, his miracles, and the judgments he pronounced' **(Ps. 105:5).**

First Half:

1. Describe why God created us to play?

2. What is discretionary time?

3. Throughout history Christians have been able to shape society for the better: give a few examples?

4. For good and bad we can trace the spread of sport around the globe. Give a few examples of how sport has spread around the world.

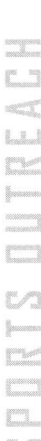

Session 2

 **Second Half:**

1. The inventor of basketball said, 'it was not what the boy did with the ball that really mattered, but what the ball did to the boy'. Agree or disagree? Discuss.

2. The church has a tendency to retreat or abdicate responsibility from a culture. We are meant to be 'salt and light', what does that mean for Christianity and modern sport?

3. Sport can be seductive and you can easily lose your perspective. When a good thing becomes a god thing, it becomes a bad thing (an idol) – a God substitute. What are some God substitutes?

4. How do we keep God number one in our life and our sports ministry?

 **Instant Replay:**
Some form of sport has influenced our lives from the beginning of time. The church engaged in sport, disengaged in sport and re-engaged. History shows that when we are not careful our methods will take over our message. That is why our next session will help us and our ministry keep a firm foundation.

Action Plan:

Memory verse:
'Remember the wonders he has done, his miracles, and the judgments he pronounced' **(Ps. 105:5).**

Challenge:
Keeping your objectives clear and in order is important to leadership. List a few goals you would like to achieve in sports ministry and share them with the Team next week. Read Chapter 3 of *Sports Outreach: Principles and Practice*.

Session 3: Biblical Foundations

Game Plan:
This session's aim is to stress that sports ministry needs to be based solely on God's Word.

Review: We see from history that when the church loses sight of its Biblical mandate, sports ministry goes off the rails.

Focus:
'Oh, that their hearts would be inclined to fear me and keep all my commands always, so that it might go well with them and their children forever!' **(Deut. 5:29).**

First Half:

1. Charles Spurgeon said 'a Bible which is falling apart usually belongs to someone who is not'. What did he mean?

2. A top athlete certainly wouldn't take to the playing fields, court, rinks or rings without confidence and the desire to do his best, neither should we go into ministry lightly. Why not?

Session 3

3. When you are reading scripture, ask yourself: (page 37, *Sports Outreach: Principles and Practice*)

Who is being _____.
Who is _____.
_____ are they?
What is the _____ of this address.
How does these scriptures _____ to me.

Read John 21 and break down the narrative using the above criteria.

 **Second Half:**

From the above illustration on page 12:
1. Describe man's relationship to God?

2. What are some of the consequences of sin?

3. Describe some of the aspects of God's grace?

4. Describe how we as Christians have been commissioned?

5. In 2 Corinthians 5, it says we are ambassadors. What does a Christian ambassador do?

Instant Replay:
Aren't you glad God gave us a book! It is full of lessons on how God in His infinite love has redeemed us and commissioned us to bring glory to Him. Our next session will help us use what we learn effectively. I love a short-cut!

Action Plan:

Memory verse:
'Oh, that their hearts would be inclined to fear me and keep all my commands always, so that it might go well with them and their children forever!' **(Deut 5:29).**

Challenge:
Make scripture reading a life long habit, this week set some Bible reading goals. Read Chapter 4 of *Sports Outreach: Principles and Practice*.

Session 4: Fast Track
Are there any shortcuts?

Game Plan:
We all love short cuts, doing things faster or easier. This session's aim is to discover if there really are shortcuts to successful sports ministry.

Review
God has given us this incredible book. It gives us meaning, purpose and direction.

Focus:
'If a man cleanses himself from the latter, he will be an instrument for noble purposes, made holy, useful to the Master and prepared to do any good work' **(2 Tim. 2:21)**.

First Half:

1. There are no shortcuts to successful sports ministry. Agree or Disagree? Explain in your own words.

2. Can you measure success in ministry, yes or no?

3. What does it mean to beat on trees with axe handles?

4. To fast track is to do your sports ministry supernaturally, not naturally.
In your own words what does that mean?

 **Second Half:**

1. Name six ways to have spiritual success.

2. For each of the above entries, give one or two practical examples of how you can have spiritual success in sports ministry.

 **SPA:**

Take the personal fitness test.
Read 1Timothy 3:1-7
Am I excited about spending time with God?
Do I read the Bible regularly?
Can I clearly share the Gospel one on one?
Am I out of sorts with anyone?
Am I enjoying the company of growing Christians?
Am I actively seeking a life of integrity and purity?

What are some of my motives for engaging in sports ministry? List four.
1.
2.
3.
4.

Do I want to be involved in the lives of sports people?

How much time can I give this initiative?

Have I really counted the cost of this initiative?

How many years am I willing to commit to Sports Ministry in this community?

Define success in sports ministry?

What are my strengths?

What are my weaknesses?

Session 4

Rate yourself on a scale from 1 – 10.

    Not very good 1—2—3—4—5—6—7—8—9—10 very good!

Am I adaptable?
    Not very good 1—2—3—4—5—6—7—8—9—10 very good!
Am I good with people?
    Not very good 1—2—3—4—5—6—7—8—9—10 very good!
Am I dependable?
    Not very good 1—2—3—4—5—6—7—8—9—10 very good!
Am I good at following through with a plan?
    Not very good 1—2—3—4—5—6—7—8—9—10 very good!
Am I good at assuming responsibility with a group?
    Not very good 1—2—3—4—5—6—7—8—9—10 very good!
Am I good at expressing myself?
    Not very good 1—2—3—4—5—6—7—8—9—10 very good!
Am I good at confronting?
    Not very good 1—2—3—4—5—6—7—8—9—10 very good!
Am I good at working up front?
    Not very good 1—2—3—4—5—6—7—8—9—10 very good!
Am I good working behind the scenes?
    Not very good 1—2—3—4—5—6—7—8—9—10 very good!
Am I a good planner?
    Not very good 1—2—3—4—5—6—7—8—9—10 very good!
Am I a good finisher?
    Not very good 1—2—3—4—5—6—7—8—9—10 very good!
Am I good at challenging myself?
    Not very good 1—2—3—4—5—6—7—8—9—10 very good!
Am I good at learning new skills?
    Not very good 1—2—3—4—5—6—7—8—9—10 very good!
Am I good with authority figures?
    Not very good 1—2—3—4—5—6—7—8—9—10 very good!
Am I good working with children?
    Not very good 1—2—3—4—5—6—7—8—9—10 very good!
Am I good working with teenagers?
    Not very good 1—2—3—4—5—6—7—8—9—10 very good!
Am I good working with adults?
    Not very good 1—2—3—4—5—6—7—8—9—10 very good!

In light of I Timothy 3:1 has this questionnaire disqualified me from leadership?

If you answered yes, ask yourself, what can I do to qualify myself for leadership?

How can I start doing sports ministry?

Have I lied to myself in the survey? If yes, start again!

Instant Replay:
We cannot measure success in the world's terms, but that does not mean that we were not called to do our best and expect God to use us greatly. We were not called to beat on trees with axe handles! Our next five sessions – Five Principles of Sports Ministry – gives us principles that will help determine our ministry.

Action Plan:

Memory verse:
'If a man cleanses himself from the latter, he will be an instrument (weapon) for noble purposes' **(2 Tim. 2:21).**

Challenge:
This week examine your life and where you come up short, ask God for forgiveness and purity. Next ask how can I be used as a weapon for God?

Read: Introduction of Section 2 and Chapter 5 of *Sports Outreach: Principles and Practice.*

18

SPORTS OUTREACH

Session 5: Principle 1
Proclamation
The verbalisation of truth

Game Plan:
From scripture we draw five principles that we can use to develop a long-term sports ministry. The first principle 'Proclamation' – sharing the good news of Jesus Christ – can be transmitted in fun and creative ways.

Review:
To be useful and successful we must stay pure and in tune with Christ.

Focus:
'How, then, can they call on the one they have not believed in? And how can they believe in the one of whom they have not heard? And how can they hear without someone preaching to them? And how can they preach unless they are sent? As it is written, 'How beautiful are the feet of those who bring good news!'" **(Rom. 10:14-15).**

Session 5

 **First Half:**

1. In the introduction to section two, Five Principles of sports ministry, I introduced the jar illustration. What does the jar represent?

2. Could the jar represent other things?

3. What do the balls represent?

4. There are five important principles to instil into your sports ministry.
   P _____
   D _____
   M _____
   R _____
   S _____

5. We can easily be sidetracked and fill our lives with less important things. What less important things have a tendency to fill our lives?

6. How do we keep the 'important things' at the heart of our lives?

7. Principle 1: Proclamation: The verbalization of truth.
Evangelism is arguably the most written about and least practised subject in Christendom. Explain.

8. A non-proclaiming Christian is a contradiction in terms. Agree or disagree.

9. When a ministry shifts from a Biblical emphasis on personal salvation to a primary focus on social issues the organization can not reproduce itself. Give four reasons for this.
   a.
   b.
   c.
   d.

10. Explain the difference between **method** and **message**.

11. Often we seem to worship the method and care little for the message. Why is that?

12. What are some methods that have become barriers to the message?

 **Second Half:**

1. What is the difference between a formal and an informal proclamation of the gospel?

2. Give four examples of each:
Formal:
   a.
   b.
   c.
   d.
Informal:
   a.
   b.
   c.
   d.

3. In your own experience have you been impacted more by an informal or a formal proclamation of the gospel?

4. What are the six benefits of a formal proclamation of the gospel?
   a.
   b.
   c.
   d.
   e.
   f.

5. You can bring a horse to water but you can't make him drink; but you can put salt in his fodder and make him mighty thirsty. What made you thirsty for Christ?

6. When we share our faith one-on-one many questions will arise. In your experience of sharing your faith what questions have emerged?

Session 5

Instant Replay:

Like beggars showing other beggars where the food is: we are to learn and become skilled at sharing God's good news. Our next session will reveal the power of both talking the talk and walking the walk.

Action Plan:

Memory verse:
'How, then, can they call on the one they have not believed in? And how can they believe in the one of whom they have not heard?' **(Rom. 10:14).**

Challenge:
God doesn't command sinners to go to church but he does command the church to go to sinners. Think about how you can best bring the gospel of Christ to those around you. Read Chapter 6 of *Sports Outreach: Principles and Practice*.

Session 6: Principle 2
Demonstration
The visualisation of truth

Game Plan:
Let's examine the best way to open up the opportunities for 'Proclamation' – through the demonstration of our faith.

Review:
We have this great inheritance as believers adopted into his family, with that inheritance comes a commission – a calling.

Focus:
'Jesus replied: "Love the Lord your God with all your heart and with all your soul and with all your mind." This is the first and greatest commandment. And the second is like it: "Love your neighbor as yourself"' **(Matt. 22:37-39).**

First Half:

1. 'The best way to teach a concept is by modelling it' (Harvard Business School). Give an example of someone who has modelled the Christian faith for you.

Session 6

2. In Matthew 7 Jesus says, 'by their fruit you will recognize them'. What is the fruit Jesus is talking about?

3. Why is it hard to be a phoney Christian in the world of sport?

 **Second Half:**

1. In your own words, explain the illustration on making tea (page 68 *Sports Outreach: Principles and Practice*).

2. We all have a tendency to gravitate to our strengths, give a few illustrations from the world of sport where athletes need to be balanced.

3. What are a few tasks that you gravitate to and what are a few tasks that you are repelled from?
-
-
-
-

4. Do you gravitate towards demonstration or proclamation?

5. Name six ways we can demonstrate God's love and redemption in our sports (recreation) community.
a.
b.
c.
d.
e.
f.

 **SPA:**

- Are my actions speaking louder than my words?
- Do my team-mates know that I am a Christian?
- Do my actions change when there is another Christian around?
- Do I understand my strengths and weaknesses?
- Do I stretch myself or stay in my 'comfort zones'?
- Am I open to developing my weaknesses?

 **Instant Replay:**
In this world of phoneys we need to see the genuine article – the real deal. If we do not demonstrate God's love in practical ways we will slash the throat of the gospel message. Our next session will help challenge us to go and encourage others *to the next level.*

Action Plan:

Memory verse:
'Jesus replied: "Love the Lord your God with all your heart and with all your soul and with all your mind." This is the first and greatest commandment. And the second is like it: "Love your neighbor as yourself"' **(Matt. 22:37-39).**

Challenge:
Examine your strengths and weaknesses; ask yourself 'how can I develop other areas of my life?' And do the dishes this week! Read Chapter 7 of *Sports Outreach: Principles and Practice.*

Session 7: Principle 3
Maturation
The cultivation of truth

Game Plan:
To examine three ingredients to nourish spiritual maturity, to provide all that is necessary for growth: Incubation, Education and Application.

Review:
Sharing and demonstrating God's love go hand in hand. Both are necessary for the seed of truth to take root. This next session will help you understand how to help Christians grow.

Focus:
'To prepare God's people for works of service, so that the body of Christ may be built up until we all reach unity in the faith and in the knowledge of the Son of God and become mature, attaining to the whole measure of the fullness of Christ' **(Eph. 4:12-13).**

 **First Half:**

1. What are some key ingredients in creating a mature professional sports person (pick a sport)?
   -
   -
   -
   -

2. Explain the three ingredients for spiritual maturity in your own words.

Incubation_____

Education_____

Application_____

3. Pick three top athletes in three different sports. How many hours a day do they prepare for competition?

4. Why is the 'maturity principle' less glamorous than the 'proclamation principle'?

5. Setting up a system for growing Christians is key and should be implemented from the beginning of your sports ministry. Agree or disagree, explain.

6. You do not get quality disciples without quantities of time. Agree or disagree?

7. How do you get quality time?

8. Describe what a quality disciple might look like.

9. Incubation is time and climate: describe a quality climate conducive for spiritual growth.

10. What are some of the examples of quality time Jesus spent with his disciples?

Session 7

11. John 8:31,32 In your own words what did Jesus mean by hold on to my teaching?

12. Education protects us from what?

 **Second Half:**

1. If we are not students of the word, how do we expect those we are trying to encourage to be?
Your shortcomings usually effect your ministry, what does that mean?

2. We should teach the Bible with: (page 79, *Sports Outreach: Principles and Practice*)
-
-
-
-
-

3. In the illustration on page 28, where in the stadium is:
   - An agnostic?
   - A seeker?
   - A Bible 'Fat-head'?
   - A young Christian?
   - A backslider?
   - A mature Christian?

4. Give an example of the first time you competed in your favourite sport. Have you improved?

5. If we don't apply what we've learned from scripture, will we improve?

6. You'll find plenty of spectators in the church but we were called to action. What are some of the benefits of applying what you learn?

7. From page 81 (*Sports Outreach: Principles and Practice*) how can you build 'Field Trips' into your sports ministry?

 SPA:

Ask yourself:
- Do I provide opportunities for ministry?
- Am I learning new insights from scripture?
- Am I giving my best in preparation or just winging it?
- Have I gone to a conference lately?
- Am I rehashing the same old lessons?
- Am I intimidated when a more knowledgeable Bible teacher is in the room while I am giving a lesson?
- Do I just teach principles or do I give concrete application to my teaching?
- Am I encouraging others to use their gifts or merely wanting them to be impressed with mine?

Session 7

Instant Replay:
We want those that God has given us to take root and grow strong. Only dead things don't grow. Our next principle helps keep the faith going and going.

Action Plan:

Memory verse:
'To prepare God's people for works of service, so that the body of Christ may be built up until we all reach unity in the faith and in the knowledge of the Son of God and become mature, attaining to the whole measure of the fullness of Christ' **(Eph. 4:12-13).**

Challenge:
We don't want our ministry to be weeds but old oak trees. Turn your ideas into action. This week ask God to show you how you can nurture a young Christian into a strong Christian. Read Chapter 8 of *Sports Outreach: Principles and Practice.*

Session 8: Principle 4
Reproduction
To Reproduce Reproducers

Game Plan:
The aim of this session is examine how all Christians are called to win, build and send God's Kingdom builders. What reliable people can I invest in?

Review:
We need to create a balanced ministry that gives opportunities for seekers to hear the 'Proclamation' of the gospel as well as give young Christians opportunity to grow and mature spiritually. The next step is to turn followers into leaders.

Focus:
'And the things you have heard me say in the presence of many witnesses entrust to reliable men who will also be qualified to teach others' **(2 Tim. 2:2).**

First Half:
We are to reproduce ourselves.

I. If you are going to go on a journey, it is good to have a destination in mind. So, why did I write, 'begin with the beginning in mind'?

Session 8

2. How many on this Team have been spiritually mentored?

3. Jesus mentored his top twelve guys. In your own words, give some examples of how he did it.

4. Who are four people you could be pouring your life into right now?
   a.
   b.
   c.
   d.

 SPA

Let's say you live to be 80 years old. (Forgive this illustration if you're over 80)
1. On the chart below tick where you want to be spiritually when you are 80?
2. Circle where you are now.
3. Ask yourself, how you are going to get to where you want to be?
4. The Holy Spirit equips all of us with unique gifts to build His kingdom. His kingdom is made out of people. If God wants you to build people for his kingdom where are those people right now on this survey?
5. How can you help them get to where God wants them to be?

selfish————————————————————————————generous
hateful—————————————————————————————loving
biblically ignorant——————————————————full of wisdom
bitter———————————————————————————————joyful
ashamed of Jesus————————————————outspoken about Jesus
stubborn——————————————————————————————secure
indifferent———————————————————————— compassionate
fearful——————————————————————————————peaceful
spiritually shallow—————————————————— spiritually rich
intolerant———————————————————————————patient
miserable———————————————————————————— Kind
violent——————————————————————————————gentle
out of Control———————————————————————self controlled
lonely—————————————————————have a wealth of friends

Second Half:

1. The goal of the leader in ministry is to reproduce reproducers, to create leaders. How can you build leadership into your sports ministry?

2. Give a few examples of coaches who have built up their team and passed on the baton in an honourable way.

3. If you leave a ministry that is strong and the ministry gets stronger, you have built leaders.
Agree or Disagree.

> 'Now Joshua son of Nun was filled with the spirit of wisdom because Moses had laid his hands on him. So the Israelites listened to him and did what the LORD had commanded Moses' **(Deut. 34:9).**

If you read the book of Joshua you will see that although Joshua's ministry was not easy, he was prepared for the challenge God gave him. How can we prepare our young leaders?

Instant Replay:
God has given us this life to use for Him. When we reproduce reproducers we are maximising our precious time. Next session – living for Christ under pressure!

Action Plan:

Memory verse:
'And the things you have heard me say in the presence of many witnesses entrust to reliable men who will also be qualified to teach others.' **(2 Tim. 2:2).**

Challenge:
Ask God to give you one or two special people that you can encourage and challenge. Read Chapter 9 in *Sports Outreach: Principles and Practice*.

Session 9: Princple 5
Sportsmanship

Game Plan:
The old cliché still works: 'It is not whether you win or lose but how you play the game'. To compete with passion and a desire to win are clearly compatible with sportsmanship.

Review: A person is physically mature when they can reproduce a child that will eventually reproduce another child. A person is spiritually mature when they can reproduce a Christian that can reproduce another Christian.

Focus:
'*Similarly, encourage the young men to be self-controlled. In everything set them an example by doing what is good. In your teaching show integrity, seriousness and soundness of speech that cannot be condemned, so that those who oppose you may be ashamed because they have nothing bad to say about us*' **(Titus 2:6-8).**

 **First Half:**

1. Paul says in Titus, 'In everything set them an example of doing what is good'. Are there exceptions or does 'in everything' mean everything?

2. Why do so many people leave their Christianity on the sidelines during competition?

3. Have you ever been guilty of putting sport above your Christian behaviour? When? Why? What happens?

4. What happens when there is no sportsmanship in sport?

 **Second Half:**

1. Why is self-sufficiency such a danger in the Christian faith?

2. What good lessons can we learn from sport?
   -
   -
   -
   -

3. Give examples from your own experience on how the seven virtues can be valuable in the world of sport.

4. How do we instil sportsmanship into our sports ministry?
   a.
   b.
   c.
   d.

 **Instant Replay:**
Time and truth walk hand in hand. All the top sports people that are respected are remembered more for their character than their achievements. Model good sportsmanship and it will reveal more about you than a cheap victory. Next session is where the rubber meets the road, putting ideas into action: Strategy Formation

Action Plan:

Memory verse:
'Similarly, encourage the young men to be self-controlled. In everything set them an example by doing what is good' **(Titus 2:6).**

Challenge:
This week examine your attitude during competition; if you have a problem ask another team-mate to help you stay 'self-controlled'. Read chapter 10 and 11 in *Sports Outreach: Principles and Practice*.

Session 10: Strategy Formation Principles that determine objectives

Game Plan:
The aim of this session is to create objectives that will shape your activities. The Four Step Survey will help you assess your time restraints, the specific needs in your community and how to best shape a programme with long-term value.

Review:
What Would Jesus Do? (W W J D) in competition? 'Go and do likewise'.

Focus:
'But those who plan what is good find love and faithfulness' (**Pro. 14:22**).

First Half:

1. What are some problems with the Lone Ranger approach to sports ministry?

2. How can you best build a team in your local 'faith community'?

3. 'A goal not written down is merely a wish.'
Agree / Disagree? Explain.

4. Are your 'senior leaders' behind your ministry?
(See Appendix 2, page 157, for ideas on how to cast vision to your church.)

Second Half:

Over the last decade, we have seen many sports ministries lose their vitality and direction because there was little thought given to long-term planning. Quite often leaders blindly pour all their energy into a church activity only to find their investment in time, energy, people, and funds, have had little return. Their activities were not achieving their objectives.

1. Give some examples of ministries that have folded because their activities did not achieve their objectives.
  -
  -
  -

2. Study the podium illustration carefully. To create an intentional long-term ministry:
   1. Start with a strong Biblical foundation.
   2. Draw Biblical principles from the scriptures.
   3. From these principles draw out key objectives you think you can apply to your ministry.
   4. From these objectives, develop and plan your activities.

 SPA

Getting Ministry from the Alpha to the Omega

Familiarize yourself with the Models of Sports Ministry in Chapter Eleven. These models will fuel ideas which will help you formulate your own ministry programme.

Step 1:
Review all five principles and ask your team:
   Which of the five principles will be the hardest to implement?
   Which of the five principles will be the easiest to implement?

Step 2:
Team ministry formation survey: (page 112, *Sports Outreach: Principles and Practice*)
Complete the survey together.

*Note between Steps 3 and 4, it may useful to take a break and digest your ideas and possible activities before you complete Step 4.

Step 3:
Transforming principles into action:
Dream big dreams! (NOTE: we plan too much in one year and not enough in four)
- In a healthy climate conducive to spiritual growth, with the help of the Holy Spirit where could a new Christian be in four years?
- Why is long term planning so important?
- Why is the illustration of the bamboo tree (page 114, *Sports Outreach: Princples and Practice*) relevant to step three? Discuss

Step 4:
Refining our objectives
The process of refining your objectives will help you to better measure the feasibility of some of your original ideas.
Develop a four-year programme: (See page 116, *Sports Outreach: Principles and Practice*)

Instant Replay:
Save your survey and watch how God will hone and use your plans for His purposes. Great job!

 **Action Plan:**

Memory Verse:
'But those who plan what is good find love and faithfulness' **(Pro. 14:22).**

Challenge:
'Run the race'

Conclusion

Building the bridge from the pitch to the pew:
'We do sport and we do church but how do we get them together?' This is one of the biggest questions in sports ministry. Sport builds fantastic relationships; but sport does not build Christians. Implementing all five principles is important. Chapter Eleven in *Sports Outreach: Principles and Practice* will give you a number of fantastic field-tested ideas on how to build vibrant relationships and create 'points of entry' with the gospel. These events are fantastic and help build trust. Jesus was great at 'meeting people where they were' and creating trust. But there was a time when he said: **'FOLLOW ME'** – **'Let the dead bury the dead'** – **'FOLLOW ME'**. Some chose to follow, others went away sad. Let me challenge you to bring people to a point of decision to follow Christ.

We have found after building relationships, proclaiming Christ and demonstrating Christ's love a few will respond to the challenge of investigating Christ further. This is the missing link – the bridge. The best way to integrate your people from the pitch (field) to the pew is a small group. Create into your 'Big Events' time in your annual programme for relaxed opportunities to explore the claims of Christ. That is why we developed **Discovery Teams** and **Impact Teams**; these are great opportunities to bring athletes together to discover the realities of Christ. *Alpha Course* or *Christianity Explored* are also fantastic courses that Sports Outreach highly recommends. Build these strategic courses into your calendar and 'Seek first His Kingdom'. Challenge your friends to, 'come on – let's follow Jesus'.

Introduction to Sports Outreach Teams (Small Groups)

The Sports Outreach Team meeting is the heart of the whole ministry concept. A 'Sports Outreach Team' is like a 'huddle': an American football term whereby a team gathers together on the pitch in a small circle and discusses various plays and strategy. A Sports Outreach Team meeting is a small group committed to investigate the scriptures in the context of their sport and life:

We have a series of three team meetings:

Sports Outreach: Discovery Teams
Sports Outreach: Impact Teams
Sports Outreach: Leadership Teams

- **Discovery Teams are geared for groups and individuals intersted in investigating the claims, challenges and teachings of Christ.**
- **Impact Teams aim to challenge and develop the believer into a stronger walk in Christ.**
- **Leadership Teams seek to challenge and train Christians to be active and fully committed followers of Christ: able to reproduce reproducers and lead Discovery and Impact Teams.**

Research suggests that most people from unchurched backgrounds attribute their conversion to Christianity by the influence of a Christian friend – relationships. Sport provides an excellent way of making friends and building relationships, these can be developed into evangelistic opportunities.

Small group meetings link the 'Big Events' and Camps into a series of consistent opportunities for proclaiming God's word and encouraging spiritual growth. Many of us have been to outreach functions where we have seen youth and adults indicate that they have trusted Christ as Lord and Savior. What an exciting time to see those for whom we have been praying apparently open up their hearts to Christ.

However, joy can turn to disappointment as we realize that not all the youth that have made a profession of faith are growing in their relationship to Christ. Why do some seem to wilt on the vine? Possibly many causes, but all too often the problem is lack of carry-on or follow-up from more mature Christians.

The church is seeing the value in having a ministry to the sports world. 'It's a knock-out', five-a-side's, and pool parties have been part of the arsenal of every youth group for years. But what comes next? Often a young person whose whole life revolves around sport will be discontent with the youth group or club geared to music or drama. Sports OutreachTeams focus on presenting Christ's salvation and His Lordship in a way that interests people in the world of sport.

The Hows, Whens, Wheres and Whos

How often should we meet?
The answer to this question varies. Some group leaders will want to meet every week while others will meet once or twice a month. Whatever you do, plan the meetings well and be consistent.

When do Sports Outreach Teams meet?
Again the answer is varied. Whether you meet after church, during club time, lunch, evenings, after school, before training or after training, early mornings before work, or Saturdays after a round of golf. Survey your group and choose the best possible time.

Where should we meet?
Many Christian groups are successful because they meet at their local church or school property in a central location. Still others like having a place that is away from church or school, the atmosphere can be less formal. Each group will have to survey their area to see which kind of setting will best accomplish their goals – to lead athletes to Christ and help them to mature in their faith. Our best model of small groups in the United Kingdom has been the Alpha Course and Christianity Explored. Many of their meetings are at night and centred around a meal.

Who leads the Team?
Sports Impact leaders need three criteria: to love Jesus; to love people and to love sport, and in that order! Obviously by now if you have read this far into the book you are interested in developing a sports ministry. From experience we want to encourage you to get help and prayer support. Leaders should take care not to dominate the meetings but rather, to facilitate discussion. But leadership is important for consistency and to maintain order.

In the book of Titus we find the young man Titus was left on the island of Crete to organize the Cretan Christians into churches. Over and over Paul tells Titus to encourage the Cretans 'do what is good'.

'Similarly, encourage the young men to be self-controlled. In everything set them a good example by doing what is good. In your teaching show integrity, seriousness and soundness of speech that cannot be condemned, so that those who oppose you may be ashamed because they have nothing bad to say about us' **(Titus 2:6-8).**

Tips for leading Sports Outreach Teams

- Start and finish with a prayer. Encourage the young people to pray silently or aloud if they want to.

- Think of an interesting icebreaker, story or topic of conversation to open with – about their day/the talk/sport etc.

- Have the Bible open and encourage the group to read it aloud and/or in turn.

- Present the questions in different ways, re-phrase where necessary and make them relevant/topical, maybe with a sporting example.

- Let the group give their own responses to the question, don't talk too much or always be giving them the answer. Keep it Bible-based and Christ-centred.

- Keep it short and sweet – don't be boring! If you don't enjoy it, the group probably won't either!

- Be honest and don't compromise on the truth.

- Don't make it too formal; you are their friend as much as their coach.

- Don't disappear at the end. Chat about other things, they may want to ask questions.

- Make sure you have prepared beforehand by looking at the passage, thinking of questions and praying.

- Do not preach: Our aim is to get alongside athletes and help point them to the cross.

- Jesus was a master of teaching through questions and stories.
  - These studies are meant to be deductive and inductive.
  - It is not always necessary to use sporty anecdotes; eventually you may run out of sports stories and metaphors. Feel free to bring in other stories but remember athletes have unique goals, stresses and time demands.

- Easily answered questions should be used to start with.

  - 'What's your favourite old time TV show?' usually gets a good laugh. This will enable the group to feel more confident to participate in the deeper questions.

- It is a general rule that the 'first half' questions are designed to encourage discussion; the 'second half' of the team meeting is created to introduce biblical themes. But it will rarely go that way.

- All answers are fine, but if the answers are getting too off track, the leader should feel free to answer 'That is interesting; let's talk about that later.' Then move back towards the aims of the meeting.

- The discussion should not be allowed to go off at too many tangents. Satan loves to throw in 'smoke screens' when the topic is relevant to people's needs.

- It is good to sit in a circle especially if it is a small group.
  - Any who want to sit/stand at the back should be gently encouraged to join in the group.

- Questions will eventually arise which you may not be able to answer.

- It is best not to try to bluff a way through.

- It is better to simply admit you do not know the answer and promise to get back with them at the next meeting.

- A member of the group can be encouraged to do the reading, but it should not be sprung on someone who may be embarrassed. 'How do you pronounce Abimalech?'

- Prayer should be introduced to the group slowly. A leader simply praying 'Thank you God for friends and sport, amen,' may speak much more to seekers than a long theological prayer.

- If a question is asked and there is no immediate response the leader should feel free to wait, allow a bit of time and then possibly restate the question.
  - Silence can be beneficial if it is not too long.

- The leader should never criticize or make anyone feel foolish about his or her answer to a question.
  - The leader should allow others to contribute answers to people's questions. Many times the young people's answers will be better than the leaders!

Leader's Notes

'Many of *the Samaritans from that town believed in Jesus because of the woman's testimony...*' **(John 4:39).**

We can see from the example of the Samaritan woman in John's gospel how effective testimony can be.

Whether you are a Coach or Huddle Leader, you will probably have an opportunity to speak personally about your faith and how you became a Christian.

'*Always be* prepared *to give an answer to* everyone *who asks you to give* the reason *for* the hope *that you have. But do this with gentleness* and respect' (1 Pet. 3:15).

Looking at the Bible:

Here are 3 questions you could consider to help you as you prepare any Bible study:
- What does it say?
- What does it say about God?
- What does that mean for me? How do I respond?

Use the team meetings as an opportunity to find out where the young people in your group are at spiritually – but be sensitive! You are likely to have a mixed group in which some people will never have heard the gospel and others will be committed Christians – this is both a challenge and an excellent opportunity for the young people to learn from you and each other.

You may want to start each team meeting with a short prayer and encourage the young people to be involved as the week progresses.

Session 6: Memory verse:
'Jesus replied: "Love the Lord your God with all your heart and with all your soul and with all your mind." This is the first and greatest commandment. And the second is like it: "Love your neighbor as yourself"' **(Matt. 22:37-38).**

Session 1: Memory verse:
'Therefore, since through God's mercy we have this ministry, we do not lose heart' **(2 Cor. 4:1-2).**

Session 7: Memory verse:
'To prepare God's people for works of service, so that the body of Christ may be built up until we all reach unity in the faith and in the knowledge of the Son of God and become mature, attaining to the whole measure of the fullness of Christ' **Eph. 4:12-13).**

Session 2: Memory verse:
'Remember the wonders he has done, his miracles, and the judgments he pronounced' **(Ps. 105:5).**

Session 8: Memory verse:
'And the things you have heard me say in the presence of many witnesses entrust to reliable men who will also be qualified to teach others' **(2 Tim. 2:2).**

Session 3: Memory verse:
'Oh, that their hearts would be inclined to fear me and keep all my commands always, so that it might go well with them and their children forever!' **(Deut. 5:29).**

Session 9: Memory verse:
'Similarly, encourage the young men to be self-controlled. In everything set them an example by doing what is good' **(Titus 2:6).**

Session 4: Memory verse:
'If a man cleanses himself from the latter, he will be an instrument (weapon) for noble purposes' **(2 Tim. 2:21).**

Session 10: Memory Verse:
'But those who plan what is good find love and faithfulness' **(Pro. 14:22).**

Session 5: Memory verse:
'How, then, can they call on the one they have not believed in? And how can they believe in the one of whom they have not heard? **(Rom. 10:14).**

Session 1: Challenge:
Consider your community this week and make a list of areas where sports ministry could be effective. Read chapter 2.

Session 2: Challenge:
Keeping your objectives clear and in order is important to leadership. List a few goals you would like to achieve in sports ministry and share them with the Team next week. Read Chapter 3

Session 3: Challenge:
Make scripture reading a life long habit, this week set some Bible reading goals. Read Chapter 4.

Session 4: Challenge:
This week examine your life and where you come up short, ask God for forgiveness and purity. Next ask 'how can I be used as a weapon for you?' Read: Introduction of Section 2 and Chapter 5.

Session 5: Challenge:
God doesn't command sinners to go to church but he does command the church to go to sinners. Think about how you can best bring the gospel of Christ to those around you. Read Chapter 6.

Session 6: Challenge:
Examine your strengths and weaknesses; ask yourself 'how can I develop other areas of my life?' And do the dishes this week. Read Chapter 7

Session 7: Challenge:
We don't want our ministry to be weeds but old oak trees. Turn your ideas into action. This week ask God to show you how you can nurture a young Christian into a strong Christian. Read Chapter 8.

Session 8: Challenge:
Ask God to give you one or two special people that you can encourage and challenge. Read Chapter 9

Session 9: Challenge:
This week examine your attitude during competition; if you have a problem ask another team-mate to help you stay 'self-controlled'. Read chapters 10 and 11.

Session 10: Challenge:
'Run the race'